WISE MEN
and WOMEN
STILL ADORE HIM

RUSSELL M. NELSON

**DESERET
BOOK**

Salt Lake City, Utah

Adapted from a Brigham Young University devotional address, December 2002.

DESERET BOOK is a registered trademark of Deseret Book Company.

Visit us at DeseretBook.com

ISBN: 978-1-60641-835-2

Printed in the United States of America
Artistic Printing, Salt Lake City, UT

20   19   18   17   16   15   14   13   12   11   10

At Christmastime, we remember family traditions with fondness. Our family is among the many that present a little pageant relating to the birth of the Babe of Bethlehem. The choice of the child to represent that Holy One is easy. The newest baby in the family gets the honor. Assignments for children to represent Mary, Joseph, adoring wise men, and shepherds are rotated from year to year. On one occasion, a child who held a broomstick capped with a silver star said that she had the most important role of all. When asked why, she replied with great conviction, "I helped the people find Jesus!"

Our "innkeepers" have been interesting to watch through the years. Some have firmly stated, "There is no room at the inn." Another lad couldn't make himself recite those lines. With the soft heart of a compassionate child, he said, "There is no room here at the inn, but you could stay at my home."

The Christmas story has a unique language. It speaks of an inn, a manger, swaddling clothes, and a virgin bearing a child.

Such terms are rarely spoken in ordinary conversation. While we remember the birth of this Holy Child, we see it as a prelude to the supernal mortal mission of the Lord Jesus Christ. Ultimately, it is His mission—the Atonement—that gives His birth its fullest meaning. He came to enable the work and glory of His Father, to bring to pass the immortality and eternal life of man (see Moses 1:39).

Because of Him, immortality became a reality for us all. After death, each body will be resurrected and reunited with its spirit to become an immortal soul (see D&C 88:14–16). And because of Him, eternal life became a possibility for us all. Eternal life is the kind of life that God lives. We qualify for that glorious gift by obedience to the ordinances and covenants of the gospel, including the endowment and sealing ordinances of the temple. Eternal life allows us to dwell in His holy presence with our families forever.

As one of the Twelve Apostles, I can say that we cherish the privilege of teaching and testifying of our beloved Savior. We gladly share our testimony of His life, His ministry, and His mission in mortality.

We commemorate His humble birth at this time of year, even though we know it did not occur in December. More likely, the Lord was born in April. Both scriptural and historical evidence suggest a time in the spring of the year, near the Jewish Passover (see D&C 20:1).

Scriptures declare that His mother Mary was espoused to Joseph (see Matthew 1:18; Luke 1:27; 2:5). They had participated in the first of two components of a Jewish marriage ceremony. Their espousal might be likened to an engagement in today's culture, which is followed later by the second component of the actual marriage ceremony.

Luke's account records the appearance of the angel Gabriel to Mary when she first learned of her mortal mission. The text reads: "Hail, thou that art highly favoured . . . blessed art thou among women. . . .

"And the angel said unto her, Fear not, Mary: for thou hast found favour with God.

"And, behold, thou shalt conceive in thy womb, and bring forth a son, and shalt call his name Jesus.

"He shall be great, and shall be called the Son of the Highest" (Luke 1:28, 30–32). Note the capital 'S' and 'H'. Our Heavenly Father is the *Highest*. Jesus is the *Son* of the *Highest*.

"Then said Mary unto the angel, How shall this be, seeing I know not a man?" (Luke 1:34).

"And the angel answered and said unto her, The Holy Ghost shall come upon thee, and the power of the Highest shall overshadow thee: therefore also that holy thing which shall be born of thee shall be called the Son of God" (Luke 1:35).

Before Joseph and Mary came together, she was expecting that holy child. Joseph desired to protect her privacy (see Matthew 1:18–19), hoping to spare Mary the punishment meted out to a woman pregnant without a completed marriage. While he pondered these things, the angel Gabriel appeared to Joseph, saying, "Joseph, thou son of David, fear not to take unto thee Mary thy wife: for that which is conceived in her is of the Holy Ghost.

"And she shall bring forth a son, and thou shalt call his name Jesus: for he shall save his people from their sins" (Matthew 1:20–21).

Mary and Joseph did not need to be taught the deep significance of the name *Jesus.* The Hebrew root from which it was derived, *Jehoshua,* means "Jehovah is salvation." So the work of the Lord God Jehovah, soon to be named Jesus, was salvation. He was to become the Savior of the world.

In the Book of Mormon we read a dialogue Nephi had with an angel, who asked, "Knowest thou the condescension of God?" (1 Nephi 11:16).

Nephi replied: "I know that he loveth his children; nevertheless, I do not know the meaning of all things.

"And he said unto me: Behold, the virgin whom thou seest is the mother of the Son of God, after the manner of the flesh.

" . . . I beheld that she was carried away in the Spirit; and after she had been carried away in the Spirit for the space of a time the angel spake unto me, saying: Look!

"And I looked and beheld the virgin again, bearing a child in her arms.

"And the angel said unto me: Behold the Lamb of God, yea, even the Son of the Eternal Father!" (1 Nephi 11:17–21).

Precious insight is added by the fond and familiar story that we recount at Christmastime, as recorded in the second chapter of Luke: "And it came to pass in those days, that there went out a decree from Caesar Augustus, that all the world should be taxed" (Luke 2:1).

This was really a capitation tax, a census, an enrollment—a registration of the citizenry of the empire of Rome. King Herod had directed that people be counted in the land of their ancestors. Mary and Joseph, then living in Nazareth, had to travel southward to the city of David, a distance of approximately 90 miles, or 150 kilometers. Perhaps they traveled even farther if they had to go around the hostile intermediate province of Samaria.

Almost certainly they traveled with relatives also summoned to the land of their ancestry. This difficult travel was no doubt made with their animals, such as dogs and donkeys. They likely camped out several nights, as three to four days would have been required for that journey. Meanwhile, the time had come for the birth of the holy child.

"And she brought forth her firstborn son, and wrapped him in swaddling clothes, and laid him in a manger; because there was no room for them in the inn" (Luke 2:7).

This verse is filled with meaning, enriched by knowing a word from the original text of the Greek New Testament and understanding the culture of that time and place. The term from which "inn" was translated is *kataluma*. We don't have an equivalent word in English. The Greek prefix *kata-* (or *cata-*) means a "downward" direction. We see it in English words such as *cata*bolism, *cata*strophe, and *cata*clysm. When the prefix *kata-* is joined with *-luma*, the word signifies a place where people take a break down from their journey. In the Greek New Testament, the word *kataluma* appears in only two other passages (see Mark 14:14; Luke 22:11), translated in each instance not as "inn," but as "guestchamber."

At that time and place, an Asian inn was not like a modern Holiday Inn or a Bethlehem Marriott. A lodging place there provided accommodations for traveling caravans, including the people and their animals. Caravans stayed at what was then known (and is still known) as a *caravansary*, or a *khan*. You may

find these terms in your dictionary, each defined as an inn surrounding a court in eastern (or Asian) countries where caravans
rest at night.[1]

Such a facility was typically rectangular in shape, comprised
of a central courtyard for the animals, surrounded by walled
cubicles (katalumas) where the people rested. These cubicles al-
lowed guests to be elevated slightly above their animals, with
open doorways so that owners could watch over their animals.
The Joseph Smith Translation of Luke 2:7 indicates that there
was no room for them in the "inns," suggesting that all of the
katalumas or cubicles of the caravansary were occupied.

The thought that the innkeepers were inhospitable or even
hostile is probably incorrect. People there were no doubt then
as they are now—very hospitable. Particularly would this have
been true at a season when the normal population of Jerusalem
and neighboring Bethlehem would have been swollen with
many relatives of the local citizenry.

At an Asian caravansary, animals were secured for the night
in the center courtyard. In that courtyard would have been donkeys and dogs, sheep, possibly camels and oxen, along with all of
the animals' wastes and odors.

Because the guestchambers surrounding the courtyard were
filled, Joseph may have made the decision to care for Mary's
delivery in the center courtyard of a caravansary, along with the
animals. It is entirely possible that in such a lowly circumstance,
the Lamb of God was born.

Twice in Luke 2 reference is made to swaddling clothes (see Luke 2:7, 12). What is the meaning of the phrase "wrapped him in swaddling clothes"? I sense a significance beyond the use of an ordinary diaper or a receiving blanket. Instead of those five words in the English text, only one word is used in the Greek text of the New Testament. That word is *sparganoo,* a verb meaning "to envelop a newborn child with special cloth, strips of which were passed from side to side."[2] The cloth would probably bear unique family identification. That procedure was especially applicable to the birth of a firstborn son.

You remember the announcement of an angel at the birth of Jesus: "This shall be a sign unto you; Ye shall find the babe wrapped in swaddling clothes, lying in a manger" (Luke 2:12). The fabric of His wrappings surely would have been recognizable and distinctive.

What about the manger? French speakers will recognize that *manger* means "to eat." A manger is a trough or an open box in a stable designed to hold feed, provender, or fodder for animals to eat. Elevated from the floor of the contaminated courtyard, a manger was probably the cleanest site available. Such a feeding trough became a cradle for our Lord!

More important than the humble place of His birth is His unique parentage. Several scriptures ask the question: "Who shall declare His generation?" (see Isaiah 53:8; Acts 8:33; Mosiah 14:8; 15:10)—meaning "Who shall declare His genealogy?" Now two millennia later, we proclaim that Jesus the Christ was born of an immortal Father and a mortal mother. From His immortal Father, Jesus inherited the power to live forever. From His mortal mother, He inherited the fate of physical death.

Jesus acknowledged these realities as they affected His own life: "No man taketh it from me," He said, "but I lay it down of myself. I have power to lay it down, and I have power to take it again. This commandment have I received of my Father" (John 10:18).

Those unique attributes of His genealogy were essential for His mission to atone for the sins of all mankind. Thus, Jesus the Christ was born to die (see 3 Nephi 27:13–15). He died that we might live again. He was born that all people could be soothed from the sting of death and live beyond the grave (see 1 Corinthians 15:55; Mosiah 16:7–8; Alma 22:14; Mormon 7:5).

His Atonement was wrought in Gethsemane, where He sweat great drops of blood (see Luke 22:44), and on Golgotha (or Calvary), where His body was lifted up upon a cross—over the place of the skull, which signified death (see 3 Nephi 27:14). This infinite Atonement would release man from the infinitude of death (see 2 Nephi 9:7). His Atonement made the resurrection a reality and eternal life a possibility for all. His Atonement became the central act of all human history.

Its importance was stressed by the Prophet Joseph Smith, who said, "the fundamental principles of our religion are *the testimony* of the Apostles and Prophets, concerning Jesus Christ, that He died, was buried, and rose again the third day, and ascended into heaven; and all other things which pertain to our religion are only appendages to it."[3]

This declaration was the undergirding inspiration that guided the First Presidency and the Quorum of the Twelve Apostles some years ago, when we were approaching the 2,000th anniversary of the birth of the Savior. We fifteen men entrusted with the keys of the kingdom prepared our written testimony. We titled it "The Living Christ: The Testimony of the Apostles." Each of the fifteen Apostles then living affixed his signature to that testimony.

Each individual with a testimony of the Lord has the privilege, in faith, to know of His divine parentage and to testify that He is the Son of the living God. True testimony includes the fact that the Father and the Son appeared to the Prophet Joseph Smith, whose birth we commemorate on December 23. That testimony includes the fact that The Church of Jesus Christ of Latter-day Saints is true, led by the living Lord, via prophecy and revelation through authorized administrators who receive and respond to direction from Him.

Even in the most troubled times of modern life, this knowledge brings us peace and joy. "Be of good cheer," the Master said, "and do not fear, for I the Lord am with you, and will stand by you; and ye shall bear record of me, even Jesus Christ, that I am the Son of the living God, that I was, that I am, and that I am to come" (D&C 68:6). Lovingly, we hold fast to His blessed promise.

Difficult days are ahead. Sin is on the increase. Paul foresaw that members of the Church would endure persecution (see 2 Timothy 3:1–13; D&C 112:24–25). Peter counseled, "If any man suffer as a Christian, let him not be ashamed; but let him glorify God on this behalf" (1 Peter 4:16). As Jesus descended below all things in order to rise above all things, He expects us to follow His example. Yoked with Him, each of us can rise above all of our challenges, no matter how difficult they may be (see Matthew 11:29–30).

Considering all that the Savior has done—and still does—for you, what can you do for Him? The greatest gift you could give to the Lord at Christmas, or at any other time, is to keep yourself unspotted from the world, worthy to attend His holy temple. And His gift to you will be the peace of knowing that you are prepared to meet Him, whenever that time shall come.

The fulness of the Master's ministry lies in the future. The prophecies of His Second Coming have yet to be fulfilled. At Christmas, of course, we focus upon His birth. And to this world He will come again. At His First Coming, Jesus came almost in secret. Only a few mortals knew of His birth. At His Second Coming, the whole of humankind will know of His return. And then He will come, not as "a man traveling on the earth" (D&C 49:22), but His glory "shall be revealed, and all flesh shall see it together" (Isaiah 40:5; see also D&C 101:23).

As a special witness of His holy name, I testify that Jesus the Christ is the divine Son of the living God. He will love you, lift you, and manifest Himself unto you, if you will love Him and keep His commandments (see John 14:21). Indeed, wise men and women still adore Him.

NOTES

1. "Caravansary" and "Khan," *Merriam-Webster's Collegiate Dictionary,* 11th ed. (Springfield, Mass.: Merriam-Webster, Inc., 2003), 184, 685.

2. See word number 4,683 in James Strong, *Abingdon's Strong's Exhaustive Concordance of the Bible* (1890), Greek Dictionary of the New Testament (Nashville: Abingdon Press, 1978), 66.

3. Joseph Smith, *Teachings of the Prophet Joseph Smith,* comp. Joseph Fielding Smith (Salt Lake City: Deseret Book, 1976), 121; also *Teachings of the Presidents of the Church: Joseph Smith* (Salt Lake City: The Church of Jesus Christ of Latter-day Saints, 2007), 49; emphasis added.

ABOUT THE AUTHOR

RUSSELL M. NELSON is a member of the Quorum of the Twelve Apostles of The Church of Jesus Christ of Latter-day Saints. Prior to his call, he was a world-renowned cardiovascular and thoracic surgeon, medical researcher, and educator. He received his B.A. and M.D. degrees from the University of Utah and a Ph.D. from the University of Minnesota. He and his wife, the late Dantzel Nelson, are the parents of ten children. Dantzel Nelson passed away in February 2005. Elder Nelson married Wendy L. Watson, a professor of marriage and family therapy in BYU's School of Family Life, in 2006.